Congress United States

Proceedings had in the Senate and House of representatives

April 23, 1880

Congress United States

Proceedings had in the Senate and House of representatives
April 23, 1880

ISBN/EAN: 9783337151997

Printed in Europe, USA, Canada, Australia, Japan

Cover: Foto ©Suzi / pixelio.de

More available books at **www.hansebooks.com**

PROCEEDINGS

HAD IN

THE SENATE AND HOUSE OF REPRESENTATIVES,

APRIL 23, 1880,

ON THE OCCASION OF

PRESENTATION OF THOMAS JEFFERSON'S VRITING-DESK TO THE UNITED STATES

BY THE

HEIRS OF THE LATE JOSEPH COOLIDGE, Jr.

WASHINGTON:
GOVERNMENT PRINTING OFFICE.
1882.

014

PROCEEDINGS

IN

THE HOUSE OF REPRESENTATIVES.

MESSAGE FROM THE PRESIDENT.

A message in writing from the President of the United States was communicated to the House by Mr. Pruden, one of his secretaries.

PRESENTATION OF THOMAS JEFFERSON'S WRITING-DESK.

Mr. CRAPO. I ask unanimous consent of the House that there be taken from the Speaker's table the message of the President of the United States in reference to a memorial of Thomas Jefferson donated to the Government by its present owners, and ask that the same be read.

The message was read, as follows:

To the Senate and House of Representatives :

I have the honor to inform Congress that Mr. J. Randolph Coolidge, Dr. Algernon Coolidge, Mr. Thomas

3

Jefferson Coolidge, and Mrs. Ellen Dwight, of Massachusetts, the heirs of the late Joseph Coolidge, jr., desire to present to the United States the desk on which the Declaration of Independence was written.

It bears the following inscription in the handwriting of Thomas Jefferson:

"Thomas Jefferson gives this writing-desk to Joseph Coolidge, jr., as a memorial of his affection. It was made from a drawing of his own by Ben. Randall, cabinet-maker, of Philadelphia, with whom he first lodged on his arrival in that city, in May, 1776, and is the identical one on which he wrote the Declaration of Independence.

"Politics as well as religion has its superstitions. These, gaining strength with time, may one day give imaginary value to this relic for its association with the birth of the great charter of our independence.

"MONTICELLO, November 18, 1825."

The desk was placed in my possession by Hon. Robert C. Winthrop, and is herewith transmitted to Congress, with the letter of Mr. Winthrop expressing the wish of the donors "to offer it to the United States, that it may hereafter have a place in the Department of State in connection with the immortal instrument which was written upon it in 1776."

I respectfully recommend that such action may be taken by Congress as may be deemed appropriate with reference to a gift to the nation so precious in its history and for the memorable associations which belong to it.

RUTHERFORD B. HAYES.

EXECUTIVE MANSION, April 22, 1880.

Mr. CRAPO. I now ask that the letter of Mr. Winthrop be read.

The Clerk read as follows:

WASHINGTON, D. C., *April* 14, 1880.

MY DEAR SIR: I have been privileged to bring with me from Boston, as a present to the United States, a very precious historical relic. It is the little desk on which Mr. Jefferson wrote the original draught of the Declaration of Independence.

This desk was given by Mr. Jefferson himself to my friend the late Joseph Coolidge, of Boston, at the time of his marriage to Jefferson's granddaughter, Miss Randolph; and it bears an autograph inscription, of singular interest, written by the illustrious author of the Declaration in the very last year of his life.

On the recent death of Mr. Coolidge, whose wife had died a year or two previously, the desk became the property of their children—Mr. J. Randolph Coolidge, Dr. Algernon Coolidge, Mr. Thomas Jefferson Coolidge, and Mrs. Ellen Dwight—who now desire to offer it to the United States, so that it may henceforth have a place in the Department of State, in connection with the immortal instrument which was written upon it in 1776.

They have done me the honor to make me the medium of this distinguished gift, and I ask permission to place it in the hands of the Chief Magistrate of the nation in their name and at their request.

Believe me, dear Mr. President, with the highest respect, very faithfully, your obedient servant,

ROBT. C. WINTHROP.

His Excellency RUTHERFORD B. HAYES,
President of the United States.

Mr. CRAPO. Mr. Speaker, I now offer the following joint resolution:

Resolved by the Senate and House of Representatives of the United States of America in Congress assembled, That the thanks of this Congress be presented to J. Randolph Coolidge, Dr. Algernon Coolidge, Mr. Thomas Jefferson Coolidge, and Mrs. Ellen Dwight, citizens of Massachusetts, for the patriotic gift of the writing-desk presented by Thomas Jefferson to their father, the late Joseph Coolidge, upon which the Declaration of Independence was written.

And be it further resolved, That this precious work is hereby accepted in the name of the United States, and the same be deposited for safe-keeping in the Department of State of the United States.

And be it further resolved, That a copy of these resolutions, signed by the President of the Senate and the Speaker of the House of Representatives, be transmitted to the donors.

The joint resolution was read a first and second time.

Mr. CRAPO. Mr. Speaker, the message of the President and the letter of Mr. Winthrop, which have just been read, give the historical sketch of the relic, which by the munificent generosity of the family of the late Joseph Coolidge, of Boston, is now presented to Congress. The genuineness of this relic has been authenticated by the autograph inscription upon it by Jefferson himself, which states that this writing-desk, from drawings of his own, was made by Ben. Randall, cabinet-maker, of Philadelphia, with whom he lodged on his arrival in that city in May, 1776, and is the identical one on which he wrote the Declaration of Independence.

The resolutions which I have offered propose that this desk be deposited for safe-keeping in the Department of State. A similar resolution was adopted by Congress in 1843, upon the occasion of the presentation to the United States by a citizen of Virginia of the sword of Washington and the staff of Franklin. There is now confided to the keeping of the nation, with the sword of Washington and the cane of Franklin, the desk of Jefferson.

What memories crowd upon us with the mention of these names. Washington, the soldier, whose sword was drawn for the independence of his country; Franklin, the philosopher, the benefactor of his race, who with simple maxims pointed out the road to wealth and who disarmed the lightning and the thunderbolt; Jefferson, the accomplished and enthusiastic scholar, whose marvelous genius and masterly pen gave form to that immortal paper which proclaimed liberty to all mankind. These are names never to be forgotten. These men were the founders of the Republic. Their name and fame are secure, and in the centuries which are to follow will be treasured by a grateful and loving people among their choicest possessions.

Mr. Speaker, the nation gladly accepts and will sacredly keep this invaluable relic. The article itself may be inconsiderable, but with this simple desk we associate a grand achievement. Upon it was written the great charter of civil liberty, the Declaration of American Independence. We pay to the heroic hand who signed that wager of battle the honors which are paid to the heroes of the battle-field. It was not valor alone which secured to us self-government. The leaders in the revolt against the tyranny and the established institutions of the Old World had courage of opinion and were full of mature wisdom and incorruptible patriotism. The men who signed the paper pledging their lives, their fortunes, and their sacred honor in support of the Declaration, and who made their fearless appeal to God and the world in behalf of the rights of mankind, were both lion-hearted and noble-minded.

Upon this desk was written, in words as pure and true as the word of inspiration, that document which opened up "a new era in the history of the civilized world." Its fit resting place is with the nation's choicest treasures. It is a precious memorial of Jefferson, more eloquent and suggestive than any statue of marble or bronze which may commemorate his deeds. In accepting it in the name of the nation we recognize the elevated private character, the eminent virtue, the profound knowledge, the lofty statesmanship, and the sincere patriotism of Jefferson, and we honor him as the father of popular government and as the great apostle of liberty.

To the pledge of safe custody with which we accept this gift we join the solemn promise that with still greater fidelity we will guard the inheritance of free institutions which has come to us through the valor of Washington and the wisdom of Jefferson, and that we will faithfully transmit, undimmed and unbroken, their richest legacies—Liberty and the Union. [Great applause.]

Mr. TUCKER. Mr. Speaker, I most cordially second the resolution offered by the honorable gentleman from Massachusetts [Mr. CRAPO].

It is an interesting fact that citizens of Massachusetts, who are also descendants of the author of the Declaration of Independence, thus mingling in their veins the blood of the two most ancient Commonwealths of the Union, should present to the United States to-day this precious memento of that great paper which was written by a son of Virginia, and was supported by the powerful and fervid eloquence of an illustrious son of Massachusetts.

How wonderful and curious is the power of the imagination to infuse the immortality of human thought into this unconscious desk that felt the impress of that pen which vindicated the already existent fact of the freedom and independence of the thirteen American States! We

have long had the original paper among our
archives, and now we have the desk on which it
was written. How vividly these recall the head
and heart and hand of Jefferson, the writer; of
Adams, the advocate; and of each of those other
representatives of the original thirteen States
whose signatures to the paper have given them
an immortal fame!

The office of the true statesman is akin to that
of the poet. The statesman must interpret and
embody in words or deeds the latent thoughts,
interests, purposes, and destiny of his people.
In a great crisis, it is his to manifest to them,
and to declare to the world, in well-digested
forms, the causes of present action, and to fore-
cast the future policy of his country. Under the
inspiration of such a statesman, a people becomes
conscious of its appointed work, and labors intel-
ligently to achieve by the wisest methods the .
highest objects of national ambition.

In this sense, there was nothing new in the
Declaration of Independence. The rough jewels
of a people's thought were gathered, polished,
and set in this splendid coronet placed upon

the brow of a virgin continent by the genius of
Jefferson. From the teeming soil of his fertile
and comprehensive mind sprang fruit-bearing
thoughts for the generations following; and he
uttered them in an age and to men of simple
tastes and habits, whose heroic natures preferred
conflict to indolent submission to wrong, if by a
brave struggle freedom and independence could
be won. Their appetite for liberty had not been
perverted by the taste of luxury, nor their pas-
sion for independence corrupted by self-indul-
gence. War was needed to win liberty and independence. Luxury could have won neither;
but let us not forget it may, as it has done, cause
the loss of both after they have been gained by
patient endurance and heroic courage.

It must be remembered that the English-speak-
ing people of the Colonies were inheritors of the
muniments of Anglo-Saxon liberty, ascertained
and established in the thirteenth century by
Magna Charta, the written constitution of England, which itself declared everything to be void
that was contrary thereto; that the English revolution of the seventeenth century was our own;

that in 1623, before James I, the Pedant King, died, Virginia declared by statute, what was confirmed as fundamental law by treaty in 1651 with the commonwealth of England, that the people of Virginia could not be taxed but by the consent of her own house of burgesses; that Massachusetts in 1636, and other Colonies subsequently, approved the same vital principle; that Samuel Adams in May, 1764, in Faneuil Hall, and Patrick Henry in May, 1765, in the house of burgesses of Virginia, in solemn and defiant tones, denounced taxation by any other means as tyrannical and against law; that a congress of nine Colonies in October, 1765, proclaimed the same doctrine; that on the 14th of October, 1774, the first Continental Congress, having met September 5, 1774, *nemine contradicente*, declared that the inhabitants of the English Colonies, by the laws of nature, the principles of the English constitution, and their several charters or compacts, were "entitled to the free and exclusive power of legislation" in all cases of "taxation and internal polity" in their "several provincial legislatures," as they were not and could not be properly represented in the British Parliament; that representation and taxation must go together; that jury trial was their "great and inestimable privilege"; that the keeping a standing army in any Colony in time of peace, without the consent of its legislature, was against law; and that they claimed all of these as "their indubitable rights and liberties," and insisted they could not be altered or abridged without their own consent "in their several provincial legislatures."

And it is interesting to state further, that Mr. Jefferson had already written the preamble to the constitution of Virginia (drawn by the master hand of George Mason, of Gunsten Hall), which had been adopted on the 29th of June, 1776, in which preamble are recited the charges against the Crown and Parliament of Great Britain, with little difference of phraseology from that used in the great Declaration itself. Nor do I doubt that both were written on this mahogany desk in the city of Philadelphia. It is obvious, therefore, that the ideas embodied in the Declaration had been floating more or less distinctly in the minds of our revolutionary fathers for years before Mr. Jefferson put his hand to that formal statement of a people's thoughts. Nor must it be forgotten that in 1775 the Colonies in Congress assembled, as well as in their respective legislatures, had taken up arms for the defense of their liberties, while disclaiming any purpose to sever their political relations to Great Britain. Lexington, Concord, and Bunker Hill, Crown Point and Ticonderoga, Great Bridge, Moore's Creek, and Fort Moultrie, and other fields were stained with the blood of men fighting for their liberties against the government whose legitimate authority they still acknowledged.

But the time had come for rebellion against their government to cease and for a revolution of their government to begin. Rebellion had sought to alter the course and policy of administration, and had failed. Revolution was needed to "alter and abolish" the existing governments and to institute new governments, securing the rights and respecting the liberties of the people. Accordingly we find that Massachusetts, New

Hampshire, Connecticut, Rhode Island, North and South Carolina early in 1776 took steps to establish new governments for their respective people. In April, 1776, Massachusetts directed all of her writs to issue in the name of "the people and government of Massachusetts," and not in the name of the king. On the 15th of May, 1776, the convention of the people of Virginia met in Williamsburg, and on that day declared for a "total separation from the Crown and government of Great Britain," and on the same day instructed her delegates in Congress to propose to Congress "to declare the united colonies free and independent states, absolved from all allegiance to or dependence upon the Crown or Parliament of Great Britain." The convention on the 12th of June, 1776, adopted a declaration of rights, and on the 29th of June, 1776, a constitution, by both of which Virginia declared her complete independence.

We are thus prepared to understand why John Adams, in the debate in Congress on the resolution for a declaration of independence, offered by Richard Henry Lee, of Virginia, on the 7th of June, 1776, argued that "the question was not whether by a declaration of independence we should make· ourselves what we are not, but whether we should declare a fact which already exists"; and hence the Declaration itself affirmed that "these united colonies *are*, and of right ought to be, free and independent states; that they *are* absolved from all allegiance to the British Crown; and that all political connection between them and the state of Great Britain *is*, and ought to be, totally dissolved."

Let us now endeavor to present a brief summary of the primordial principles of American polity, formulated by the comprehensive genius of Jefferson, the true impersonation of the new era of free thought, free conscience, free commerce, free men, and a free continent.

First. Mark its denunciation of standing armies in time of peace without legislative consent, its declaration for the supremacy of the civil over the military power, for an independent judiciary, for impartial jury trial, for the bond indissoluble between representation and taxation, and for free government by and under law.

014——2

Second. Mark its clear assertion of the equality of the individual right of every man to life, liberty, and the pursuit of happiness as endowments of the Creator, not an assertion of an equality in the endowments themselves, but in the right of each to that with which his Creator has endowed him, inalienable by himself, because it would be a breach of his duty thus to relinquish the trust reposed in him, and inalienable by all others, because a violation of the right divinely vested in him.

This is the foundation stone of all individual liberty under all forms of political institutions.

Third. Note the germ of local self-government as an essential to liberty resulting from the demonstrated impracticability of good government for any people when it is controlled by another people. The power which governs must not be alien to but must be in sympathy with the interests of the government, or tyranny will be the result. It was not the tea tax or the stamp act which caused the Revolution. They were the occasions of it. They only demonstrated that it was an intolerable evil to any

people where there was a want of sympathy
between those who laid and those who paid
taxes. In the language of Burke, in his speech
on American taxation, when speaking of John
Hampden and ship money, "The payment of
half twenty shillings on the principle it was
demanded, would have made him a slave." The
tax was small: the principle was great.

> Rightly to be great
> Is not to stir without great argument;
> But greatly to find quarrel in a straw
> When honor's at the stake!
> Submission was slavery!
> Resistance was liberty!

Fourth. The declaration of the right of revolution when existing governments wholly fail to
be administered for the protection of the rights
of the people, the right of every people to mold
the form and control the administration of its
government according to their will, thus basing
all government on the consent of the governed;
the excellence of popular government of a rep-
resentative democracy—these were all clearly
indicated in this paper. And Mr. Jefferson, by his
subsequent advocacy of the freedom of the land
from the fetters of primogeniture and entails and by

his act for religious freedom, as well as by his whole life, vindicated the consistency of his devotion to the liberty of the people under a government of law restrained and guided by themselves.

Fifth. But it is impossible not to see that in the minds of Jefferson and his contemporaries there was a larger view, looking to the continental questions of international importance connected with this new era of free thought, free conscience, free commerce, and the new institutions of democratic republics.

In 1823 Mr. Jefferson wrote a letter to President Monroe upon the promulgation of the doctrine bearing the name of the latter, in which he says :

Our first and fundamental maxim should be, never to entangle ourselves in the broils of Europe. Our second, never to suffer Europe to meddle with our cisatlantic affairs.

In the debate upon the Declaration of Independence, furnished by Mr. Jefferson to Mr. Madison, and published in the first volume of the Madison Papers, there is a reference to our prospective relations with Europe which shows that the doctrine of continental independence was in the minds and hearts of the men of 1776, and as a corollary from their great Declaration it became a fixed canon of our foreign policy in 1823.

Such, Mr. Speaker, as I understand them, are some of the most important principles recalled by the presence among us to-day of this unconscious witness of the work of that remarkable man whose pen embodied the idea and purpose of the people of these States for the security of their liberty and for the independence of the American continent. Upon his tomb he left to be inscribed this, as the chief of his triple claims to the remembrance of mankind—in these words:

Thomas Jefferson, author of the Declaration of American Independence, of the statute of Virginia for religious freedom, and father of the University of Virginia.

Adams and Jefferson; sons of Massachusetts and Virginia; co-workers in the adoption of this grand charter of freedom; twin brothers of the Revolution; rival representatives of the two types of political opinion in America; after the strifes of a long political career, they passed together, in friendly reunion, into the land which is concealed from human vision, crowned with the benedictions of the people to whose liberty, independence, and welfare their lives had been patriotically consecrated.

The old thirteen have become thirty-eight States. May not the interest excited by this simple memorial inspire in the representatives of these States the renewal of the pledge of "Lives and fortunes and sacred honor," to the perpetuation of our free institutions and to the promotion of the glory of our common country, by a faithful adherence to that great Constitution, which was ordained and established to secure the blessings of liberty to ourselves and our posterity? [Prolonged applause.]

The SPEAKER. The question is on the engrossment and third reading of the joint resolution.

The joint resolution was ordered to be engrossed and read a third time; and being engrossed, it was accordingly read the third time, and passed by a unanimous vote.

The SPEAKER. The Chair will cause to be conveyed to the Senate the desk, together with the resolution passed by the House.

PROCEEDINGS

IN

THE SENATE.

MESSAGE FROM THE HOUSE.

A message from the House of Representatives, by Mr. George M. Adams, its Clerk, announced that the House had passed a joint resolution (H. R. No. 290) accepting the gift of the desk used by Thomas Jefferson in writing the Declaration of Independence ; in which it requested the concurrence of the Senate.

ACCEPTANCE OF JEFFERSON'S DESK.

The VICE-PRESIDENT. The Chair lays before the Senate a message from the President of the United States, which will be read.

The message was read, as follows :

To the Senate and House of Representatives :

I have the honor to inform Congress that Mr. J. Randolph Coolidge, Dr. Algernon Coolidge, Mr. Thomas

Jefferson Coolidge, and Mrs. Ellen Dwight, of Massachusetts, the heirs of the late Joseph Coolidge, jr., desire to present to the United States the desk on which the Declaration of Independence was written. It bears the following inscription in the handwriting of Thomas Jefferson :

" Thomas Jefferson gives this writing-desk to Joseph Coolidge, jr., as a memorial of his affection. It was made from a drawing of his own, by Ben. Randall, cabinet-maker, of Philadelphia, with whom he first lodged on his arrival in that city in May, 1776, and is the identical one on which he wrote the Declaration of Independence.

" Politics as well as religion has its superstitions. These, gaining strength with time, may one day give imaginary value to this relic for its association with the birth of the great charter of our independence.

" MONTICELLO, *November* 18, 1825."

The desk was placed in my possession by Hon. Robert C. Winthrop, and is herewith transmitted to Congress, with the letter of Mr. Winthrop, expressing the wish of the donors " to offer it to the United States, that it may hereafter have a place in the Department of State in connection with the immortal instrument which was written upon it in 1776."

I respectfully recommend that such action may be taken by Congress as may be deemed appropriate with reference to a gift to the nation so precious in its history and for the memorable associations which belong to it.

RUTHERFORD B. HAYES.

EXECUTIVE MANSION, *April* 22, 1880.

WASHINGTON, D. C., *April 14*, 1880.

MY DEAR SIR : I have been privileged to bring with me from Boston, as a present to the United States, a very precious historical relic. It is the little desk on which Mr. Jefferson wrote the original draught of the Declaration of Independence.

This desk was given by Mr. Jefferson himself to my friend the late Joseph Coolidge, of Boston, at the time of his marriage to Jefferson's granddaughter, Miss Randolph ; and it bears an autograph inscription, of singular interest, written by the illustrious author of the Declaration in the very last year of his life.

On the recent death of Mr. Coolidge, whose wife had died a year or two previously, the desk became the property of their children—Mr. J. Randolph Coolidge, Dr. Algernon Coolidge, Mr. Thomas Jefferson Coolidge, and Mrs. Ellen Dwight—who now desire to offer it to the United States, so that it may henceforth have a place in the Department of State, in connection with the immortal instrument which was written upon it in 1776.

They have done me the honor to make me the medium of this distinguished gift, and I ask permission to place it in the hands of the Chief Magistrate of the nation in their name and at their request.

Believe me, dear Mr. President, with the highest respect, very faithfully, your obedient servant,

ROBERT C. WINTHROP.

His Excellency RUTHERFORD B. HAYES,
President of the United States.

The VICE-PRESIDENT. The Chair lays before the Senate the joint resolution received from the House of Representatives.

The joint resolution (H. R. No. 290) accepting the gift of the desk used by Thomas Jefferson in writing the Declaration of Independence was read the first time by its title.

The joint resolution was read the second time at length, as follows:

Resolved by the Senate and House of Representatives, &c., That the thanks of this Congress be presented to J. Randolph Coolidge, Algernon Coolidge, Thomas Jefferson Coolidge, and Mrs. Ellen Dwight, citizens of Massachusetts, for the patriotic gift of the writing-desk presented by Thomas Jefferson to their father, the late Joseph Coolidge, upon which the Declaration of Independence was written; and

Be it further resolved, That this precious relic is hereby accepted in the name of the nation, and that the same be deposited for safe-keeping in the Department of State of the United States; and

Be it further resolved, That a copy of these resolutions, signed by the President of the Senate and Speaker of the House of Representatives, be transmitted to the donors.

The VICE-PRESIDENT. This joint resolution having been read twice, is before the Senate as in Committee of the Whole.

Mr. DAWES. Mr. President, I cannot think that the Senate will object to an interruption of its ordinary business to consider for a brief mo-

ment so interesting a subject as that contained
in the resolutions which have just come from the
House. The message of the President and the
resolutions themselves have already communicated to us so much of the history of the subject
to which they allude that little more is necessary
to put us in possession of the facts which im-
part to it an interest and value justifying these
proceedings.

This small, plain, unpolished mahogany writing-desk was once the property of Thomas
Jefferson. Why it has been preserved with
scrupulous care, and now arrests the attention
of the nation, he himself, after keeping it for
half a century, has told us in an inscription
placed upon it by his own hand in the last year
of his life, in these words :

Thomas Jefferson gives this writing-desk to Joseph
Coolidge, jr., as a memorial of his affection. It was
made from a drawing of his own, by Ben. Randall,
cabinet-maker, of Philadelphia, with whom he first
lodged on his arrival in that city in May, 1776, and
is the identical one on which he wrote the Declaration
of Independence. Politics as well as religion has its
superstitions. These, gaining strength with time, may
one day give imaginary value to this relic for its asso-

ciation with the birth of the great charter of our independence.

NOVEMBER 15, 1825.

Mr. Coolidge was the husband of a granddaughter of Mr. Jefferson. He was a resident of Boston, and has recently deceased. His children, Mr. J. Randolph Coolidge, Mr. Algernon Coolidge, Mr. Thomas Jefferson Coolidge, and Mrs. Ellen Dwight, through our distinguished fellow-citizen, the Hon. Robert C. Winthrop, now present this most remarkable relic to the United States.

Embellishment or enlargement can add nothing to this simple story. It is, of itself, enough to draw to this plain memorial the homage of mankind, and will be told to listening pilgrims and votaries in all the generations that shall count the years of the Republic and the spread of free institutions in the world. The man, the occasion, and the subject crowd in upon our thoughts and fill us with the admiration and wonder of those who look upon the place where miracles have been wrought.

The youngest and least experienced of all

his associates in practical government, none of whom had shared in anything but the affairs of a dependent colony, is called upon to commit to writing, for the judgment of all mankind and for all time, the reasons for the dismemberment of an empire and the creation of a republic among the nations of the earth. And the work thus undertaken was so accomplished, upon this writing-desk, that the test of a century of criticism and trial has only made it more clear that nothing could have been added or excluded. Constitutions based upon it have indeed been altered and amended many times, but it has always been in the endeavor to more and more conform them to the great truths enunciated in this immortal instrument. Mr. Jefferson termed it in the inscription upon this memorial, after fifty years of experience and growth, "the charter of our independence." It is more. A century of political commotion and upheaval has proven it to be the great title-deed of free institutions throughout the world.

It cannot but be that everything connected with the production of this wonderful instrument will be cherished by the American people with an almost sacred reverence, and by lovers of free institutions everywhere with the regard which draws the devout to a shrine. Let, therefore, this writing-desk, upon which it was written, be gladly accepted by the nation and carefully preserved with the great charter itself in the archives of that mighty government thus called into being. And there, with the sword of Washington and the staff of Franklin, which the nation has already accepted with reverent gratitude, let these muniments of our title be preserved evermore.

I should, Mr. President, fail altogether in my duty to the people of Massachusetts if I did not give expression at this time to their great gratification for the large share that Commonwealth has had from the beginning in all that makes this occasion proper or worthy of attention. Massachusetts and Virginia had from the outset of the Revolution conspicuously joined hands in the great struggle, sharing the obloquies and perils with which it opened on their soil. Arthur Lee, of Virginia, had, for many

years before, as the agent of Massachusetts,
pleaded her cause before the British throne.
Samuel Adams and Richard Henry Lee kindled
together the fires of the Revolution. It was on
motion of John Adams, in a most critical period
in the temper of the Colonies, that Washington himself was called to the command of the
American Armies. Mr. Adams was with Mr.
Jefferson upon the committee instructed by the
Continental Congress to draft a declaration of
independence, and joined in imposing that duty
upon one many years his junior, because of his
"reputation for a matchless felicity in embody-
ing popular ideas." That matchless felicity of
Mr. Jefferson produced the Declaration of Independence, and the peerless eloquence of John
Adams carried it through a hesitating Congress.
These distinguished patriots having each in
turn enjoyed the highest honors of the Republic they had together so conspicuously
helped to create, were both permitted by Prov-
idence to close their illustrious career on the
fiftieth anniversary of the day they had made
immortal, and to pass together to their reward

amid the shouts of a people applauding their great work.

· And now this precious relic, around which so many memories of the great actors of the Revolution cluster, kept by Virginia for fifty years and then committed by its illustrious owner to the care of Massachusetts for another half century, is to-day donated to the United States by those in whose veins commingle the blood of both these ancient Commonwealths. Thus do Massachusetts and Virginia again stand side by side amid the glories which have come down to us from the Revolution.

I hope, Mr. President, that the third reading of the resolution will be unanimously ordered.

Mr. JOHNSTON. Mr. President, as one of the Senators from the State in which Mr. Jefferson was born, it is a duty most agreeable to me to move concurrence in the resolution under consideration.

One of Mr. Jefferson's biographers describes the relic now before us as "a little writing-desk only three inches high," which has upon it this inscription placed there by Mr. Jefferson himself:

Thos. Jefferson gives this writing-desk to Joseph Coolidge, jr., as a memorial of affection. It was made from a drawing of his own, by Benj. Randall, cabinetmaker, of Philadelphia, with whom he first lodged on his arrival in that city in May, 1776, and is the identical one on which he wrote the Declaration of Independence. Politics, as well as religion, has its superstitions. These gaining strength with time may one day give imaginary value to this relic for its association with the birth of the great charter of our independence.

MONTICELLO, *November* 18, 1825.

And though he was then nearly eighty-three years old, it is written in the same bold, clear, and strong handwriting in which he penned the Declaration of Independence almost half a century before, when he was a young man, only a little more than thirty. He speaks of the superstitions of politics and of the imaginary value which may one day attach to this relic. But the reverence a free people are ready to accord to the instruments of such events as this little desk chronicles is neither superstition nor an idle and empty imagination; for on that little desk was done a work greater than any battle,

014—3

loftier than any poem, more enduring than any monument.

When the Declaration of Independence was written this earth was centuries old; many people had existed, many battles had been fought, many struggles had been made, and many patriots had lived; revolutions, rebellions, and wars for freedom had been waged, but civil liberty, as we now see, enjoy, and understand it, was still unknown. The struggles of past days had been merely for a change of actual government, and not so much for new and better principles. It was to get rid of the then ruler, but to let the new one, put in the place of the old, govern on the same platform. When Cæsar was killed the conspirators had no thought of anything but freeing the country from an overshadowing man. In their conception the only thing to be done was to give the reins into new hands. But at last came the author of the Declaration of Independence. What had been cloudy and obscure and seen dimly by others was a clear vision to him. He saw not only what the rights of a citizen were, but how to defend, guard, and protect them; not only what true civil liberty was, but how to acquire and how to preserve it. And thus our Revolution was therefore not a simple change of government for the people of the thirteen colonies; it was not the case of a dependent• territory breaking away from the mother country and enforcing the separation by arms, and then conducting its affairs upon the same old plan; nor was it only the birth of a new nation, of one government more added to those already existing; but with the establishment of this new nation came new theories, practices, and principles.

Bills of right and written constitutions declared and defined the duties, powers, and limitations of the government and the rights of the citizen.

For the divine right of kings was substituted the sacred rights of the people.

In place of the service of the serf to the baron was established a well-regulated militia and the right of the people to keep and bear arms.

Instead of privileged classes and orders of nobility all men were declared equal under the law.

The sword was the governing power in many countries, but here it was made the servant of the civil law.

Instead of subsidies levied by governments and collected by force and spent without responsibilities, no citizen here is taxed who is not represented, and no tax is levied except by the representatives of the people.

Instead of blind obedience, ignorance, and the union of church and state, "Congress can make no law respecting an establishment of religion or prohibiting the free exercise thereof, or abridging the freedom of speech or of the press, or of the right of the people peacefully to assemble and to petition the government for a redress of grievances."

And without undervaluing the great men who lived and acted with Mr. Jefferson, it is no disparagement to them to say that he was the principal actor in the events of that day. His brain originated, his hand executed. The principles he enunciated, so new then, are already old. In less than a single century they are taking root all over the world, and written constitutions and representatives of the people are now the rule in civilized nations.

Mr. President, I move the adoption of the resolution.

The joint resolution was ordered to a third reading, and read the third time.

The VICE-PRESIDENT. The resolution having had three several readings, the question is, Shall it pass?

The joint resolution was passed.

www.ingramcontent.com/pod-product-compliance
Lightning Source LLC
Chambersburg PA
CBHW021603270326
41931CB00009B/1354